A BRIEF HIST

OF

THE KING'S ROYAL RIFLE CORPS.

" Celer et Audax."

" Louisberg," " Quebec, 1759," " Martinique, 1762, 1809," " Havannah," " Roleia,"
"Vimiera," " Talavera," " Busaco," " Fuentes d'Onor, " Albuhera,"
" Ciudad Rodrigo," " Badajoz," " Salamanca," " Vittoria," " Pyrenees," " Nivelle,"
" Nive," " Orthes," " Toulouse," " Peninsula," " Punjaub," " Mooltan,"
"Goojerat," " Delhi," " Taku Forts," " Pekin," "South Africa, 1851–2-3, 1879,"
"Ahmad Khel," " Kandahar, 1880," "Afghanistan, 1878-80," "Egypt, 1882, 1884,"
" Tel-el-Kebir," "Chitral," "South Africa, 1899–1902," " Defence of Ladysmith,"
" Relief of Ladysmith."

Colonel-in-Chief :

HIS MAJESTY THE KING.

Colonels Commandant :

1st Battalion	-	Field·Marshal Rt. Hon. F. W. Lord Grenfell, P.C., G.C.B., G.C.M.G.
2nd ,,	-	Lieut.-Gen. Sir Edward T. H. Hutton, K.C.M.G., C.B.
3rd ,,	-	Major-Gen. Sir Cromer Ashburnham, K.C.B.
4th ,,	-	Major-Gen. Sir Wykeham Leigh-Pemberton, K.C.B.

REPRINTED BY PERMISSION FROM "THE KING'S ROYAL RIFLE CORPS
CHRONICLE" OF 1911, AND PUBLISHED 1912.

WINCHESTER :

PRINTED BY WARREN AND SON, LTD., 85, HIGH STREET.

From a photograph by W. & D. Downey, London.

George R. I.

Col. in Chief

CONTENTS.

MAPS.

A BRIEF HISTORY

OF

THE KING'S ROYAL RIFLE CORPS.

———

PREFACE.

THIS abridged history of the Regiment has been prepared by certain members of the History Committee, and edited by the Chairman.

The Chairman (Lieut.-General Sir Edward Hutton) is indebted to the following members of the Regimental History Committee :— Major - General Astley Terry, Major the Hon. C. Sackville-West, Captain Hereward Wake, and also to Colonel Horatio Mends for the contribution, wholly or in part, of Part I, Sec. 3; Part II, Secs. 4 and 5; Part III, Secs. 9 and 10; and Part III, Secs. 7 and 8 respectively.

The existing short history, written by Major-General Astley Terry and Colonel Mends and published with the Standing Orders of the Regiment, has been taken as a basis.

It has been the object of the compilers, while amplifying the short history, to form a Prelude to the large and comprehensive History of the Regiment by Captain Lewis Butler, the publication of which —from the difficulties to be overcome, the researches to be made, and the immense mass of detail to be dissected—must necessarily be further delayed.

Every effort has been made to narrate in a concise and popular form the origin, history, and world-wide services of the several battalions, so that every Rifleman may be able to learn at least the outlines of the

B

history of his Regiment—a Corps whose battle honours are unequalled in number, and whose reputation for discipline and courage is unsurpassed in the annals of the British Army.

The gallant exploits of the Regiment are here given in no spirit of pride or self-adulation, but with the earnest hope that, profiting by the example of their predecessors, the present and future generations of Riflemen may not only successfully maintain as a sacred trust the credit and renown of The King's Royal Rifle Corps, but may also still further add to the honours and reputation already won.

December 1st, 1911.

NOTE.—The names of Officers of the British Army who do not belong to the Regiment are printed in italics. Campaigns and battles, which have been awarded as "Battle Honours" to the Regiment, are printed in capitals.

PART   I.—1755—1824.

I.

1755–1763.—ORIGIN OF THE REGIMENT AND ITS SERVICES IN NORTH AMERICA.

ORIGIN.   The Regiment was raised during 1755–56 in North America under special conditions, for the express purpose of assisting our Army to retrieve the terrible disaster which had befallen the British troops under *General Braddock* at the hands of a smaller force of French and Red Indians in the forest fastnesses upon the banks of the Ohio River.   It had been found that the slow and ponderous movements of troops trained upon the European model, with their heavy accoutre- ments, tight uniforms, and unsuitable tactics, were helpless against savages, and almost equally helpless against soldiers habituated to wars in the dense forests and trackless wastes of America. It was therefore decided by the British Government to raise in America, from amongst the Colonists themselves, a force which should be able to meet these conditions.

Designated as the 62nd, and the following year as the 60th Royal Americans, the Regiment was accordingly formed of 4,000 men in four battalions, and General the Earl of Loudoun, Commander-in-Chief of the British Army in America, was appointed Colonel-in-Chief. It was recruited from settlers, mainly of German and Swiss origin, in the States of Massachusetts, New York, Pennsylvania, Maryland, and North Carolina, to which were added volunteers from British regiments and others. Many of the senior officers and a consider-able number of the Company officers were drawn from the armies of Europe, some of them being highly trained and experienced soldiers.

Through the bold initiative of Lieutenant-Colonel Henry Bouquet,* a Swiss officer of distinction, com-manding the 1st Battalion, the 60th Royal Americans adopted Colonial methods of equipment, simpler drill, open formations, and the Indian system of forest warfare, thus early acquiring those attributes of individual action, swift initiative, and of elastic though firm discipline, which have been the conspicuous char-acteristics of the Regiment throughout its long and brilliant career, characteristics which have made its reputation. Thus equipped, The Royal American Regi-

---

* Afterwards Brigadier-General Bouquet. Born 1719, died 1765. The victor of Bushey Run. A brilliant officer, of the highest capacity as a leader and administrator. It has been said that by his untimely death Great Britain lost a general whose presence might well have caused the American War of Independence to assume a different aspect. For biographical sketch *vide* Regimental Chronicle, 1910.

ment from its very beginning played a distinguished and memorable part in establishing British power in North America.

The great struggle between France and England for supremacy in America was at its height, when early in 1758, Abercromby,* who had succeeded Loudoun as Commander-in-Chief, decided upon a general advance.

The 1st and 4th Battalions, under Bouquet and Haldimand,† formed part of the main Army in the Western Field of operations, and on the banks of Lake
July 8th, 1758, TICONDEROGA Champlain, at the memorable defeat of Ticonderoga, "at once a glory and a shame," the 4th Battalion and a portion of the 1st showed a stubborn courage worthy of the highest praise, and lost very heavily in killed and wounded. On July the 27th, three weeks later, regardless of their losses, the Regiment furnished a part of the column under Bradstreet,‡ of the 60th, which, after a forced march, captured by a *coup de main* Fort Frontenac on Lake Ontario.

The 1st Battalion, employed on the Western frontiers under *General Forbes*, played the leading part in the
Nov. 25th, 1758, Capture of FORT DUQUESNE. advance against Fort Duquesne on the Ohio, in November, 1758, and led by the gallant Bouquet effected its capture from the French and Red Indians. This brilliant triumph over great physical difficulties was achieved by sheer determination, endurance, and pluck ; and the solid value of the victory is thus summed up by the American historian, Parkman:—
" It opened the great West to English enterprise, took from France half her savage allies, and relieved her Western borders from the scourge of Indian Wars."

* General James Abercromby, Colonel-in-Chief, 1757–1758.

† Afterwards Lieut.-General Sir Frederick Haldimand. Born 1718, died 1791. Commander-in-Chief in North America, and Governor of Quebec—a distinguished soldier-statesman.

‡ Afterwards Major-General John Bradstreet. Born 1710, died 1774 ; a successful leader of irregular troops.

Fort Duquesne, re-christened Fort Pitt, was thereupon   1758—1760.
garrisoned by a detachment of the 60th, and was
destined later to play a prominent part in the subsequent operations.

The 2nd and 3rd Battalions, under Lieut.-Colonel
Young and Major Augustine Prevost* respectively,
early in 1758 were ordered to join Generals Amherst †
and *Wolfe* in the Eastern Field of operations, and they
took a prominent part in the capture of Louisburg.   July 26th, 1758, LOUISBURG.

These two Battalions were subsequently in 1759
moved up the St. Lawrence to Quebec, where they
still further distinguished themselves at Montmorency
Falls, below Quebec, on July the 31st, and by their rapid
movements and their intrepid courage won from *General
Wolfe* the motto of " Celer et Audax " (Swift and Bold).
A still greater opportunity occurred on the 13th of
September at the decisive battle of Quebec, where   Sept. 13th, 1759, QUEBEC.
upon the Plains of Abraham the 2nd Battalion, whose
Grenadier Company had been the first to scale the
heights, covered the left during the battle against a
very superior force of Red Indians and French, who
made the most determined efforts to assail the flank
and rear of *Wolfe's* army under cover of the dense
bush and rocky ground.‡   The 60th thus lost heavily in
killed and wounded.   The 3rd Battalion played a no
less important part by holding in check the enemy,
who threatened the rear through the thick woods on
the river banks.

Amherst, who in 1759 had succeeded Abercromby   1760, MONTREAL.
in chief command of the Army, led the main force
in its advance to Montreal, where, on the 8th of

* Afterwards Major-General.   Born 1723, died 1786; dangerously wounded in
July, 1759, above Quebec ; the victor of Savannah, 1779, and a distinguished
soldier.

† Afterwards Field Marshal Sir Jeffery Amherst, Baron Amherst, Colonel-in-
Chief, 1758-1797.

‡ The Grenadier Companies also of the 2nd and 3rd Battalions were included
in the six companies composing the Louisberg Grenadiers, which occupied the
place of honor in the front line.

September, 1760, the 4th Battalion, a portion of the 1st, and the Grenadiers of the 2nd and 3rd, shared in the glories of the surrender of the French Army under the Marquis de Vaudreuil—a surrender through which the supremacy in America finally passed to the British Crown.

Following up their successes in 1758, under *Forbes*, Bouquet and the 1st Battalion had by degrees captured or occupied the whole of the French posts west of the Alleghany Mountains, and they were accordingly chosen for the arduous task of defending the various forts established in the unexplored country south of the great lakes. A region embracing thousands of miles of surface was thus consigned to the keeping of five or six hundred men—a vast responsibility for a single weak Battalion garrisoning a few insignificant forts.

In 1763 took place the general and sudden rising of the Indians under Pontiac—a formidable conspiracy, bringing ruin and desolation to the settlers in those wild regions, and even threatening the safety of the Colonies. By surprise or stratagem the Indians, in overwhelming numbers, secured many of the widely scattered posts held by the 60th, murdering some of the slender garrisons and beleaguering others. But the important posts of Fort Detroit upon the Straits joining Lake Erie and Lake Huron, and of Fort Pitt commanding the Ohio River valley, both garrisoned by the 60th under Gladwyn and Ecuyer respectively, were gallantly and successfully held against tremendous odds. The relief of these two important posts were operations of the greatest urgency, and every effort was made to get sufficient troops for this purpose.

It was at once decided that Fort Pitt on the Ohio, guarding as it did the Western frontier of the Colonies, must be saved at any cost, but owing to the reduction of the Army in America after the great war, it was with the utmost difficulty that, at Carlisle, 150 miles west of Philadelphia, a small column was formed under Bouquet, consisting of barely 500 men of the 1st Battalion 60th Royal Americans and the 42nd Highlanders. This courageous band, led by the stout-hearted and experienced Henry Bouquet, marched almost as a forlorn hope to the relief of the garrison. Reaching, after a long and weary march, the dangerous defiles of Bushey Run, ten miles only from their objective and within view of the scene of Braddock's crushing defeat, a site of battle deliberately chosen by their cunning foe, the little force was suddenly attacked by a vastly superior number of Indian braves. During two long trying days the combatants fought a desperate battle, until at last Bouquet's genius as a leader achieved a brilliant victory. This victory, pronounced by an American historian " the best contested action ever fought between white men and Indians," was followed up in the coming year by a vigorous advance by Bradstreet upon Detroit by way of Lake Erie; and by Bouquet marching from Fort Pitt with a column consisting of his own Battalion of the 60th, the 42nd, and Provincial troops, which he led into the very heart of the enemy's country. Bouquet's column was triumphant, and upon reaching the Indian settlements on the River Muskingum, deep in the wild fastnesses of the primeval forest, their leader's diplomatic skill and defiant attitude completed the successful issue of the campaign. Bouquet thus rightly earned for himself and his men the credit of having finally broken the French influence and Red Indian power in the West, giving to the British Crown all the vast territories west of the Alleghany Mountains and south of the Great Lakes, comprising now the States of Pennsylvania, Virginia, Western Virginia, Ohio, Kentucky, Indiana, Michigan, and Illinois.

1763—1764.

Aug. 5th and 6
1763.
BUSHEY RUN

Nov. 15th, 1764,
RED INDIAN
CAMPAIGN.

1762–1764.

The conspicuous part played at this period by the 60th Royal Americans, and the exceptional merit of many of its officers have hitherto been better understood in the United States and in Canada than by our own countrymen. But it is now at last acknowledged that the Regiment, owing to its especial attributes, was in the forefront of all those operations which (more than any others) added a peculiar lustre to the British Crown at this early stage of the evolution of the British Empire in North America. There is no period in the Regimental history of which The King's Royal Rifle Corps may more justly be proud than the epoch from its birth in 1755 to the final overthrow of the French and Red-Indian power in 1764.

1762, MARTINIQUE.

Meanwhile, in February, 1762, the 3rd Battalion, moving to the West Indies, had taken part in the capture of MARTINIQUE. It subsequently joined the expedition to Cuba under the *Earl of Albemarle*, where, led by Brigadier-General Haviland,* it played a leading part

Aug. 13th, 1762. HAVANNAH.

in the capture of HAVANNAH from the Spaniards on the 13th of August.

II.

1764–1807.—WEST INDIES AND THE AMERICAN WAR.

WEST INDIES.

On the termination of the French War in America the British Army was reduced, and in 1764 and 1763 respectively the 3rd and 4th Battalions were disbanded.

The discontented and hostile feeling of the American Colonies at this period rendered it advisable to transfer The Royal Americans to the West Indies, recruited as they were from the Colonists themselves. Thus it fell to the lot of the Regiment to take a prominent

---

* General William Haviland was Colonel Commandant in 1761-1762.

share in the conquest and annexation of the West Indian Islands and the adjacent coast, which took place at this period. The officers in many instances filled important posts as Governors and Administrators of the various islands.

1765–1783.

On the outbreak of the War of Independence in 1775 the 3rd and 4th Battalions were again raised in England and despatched to the West Indies, and thence to Florida, where they figured prominently in the operations in that region.

In 1779 the 3rd and some companies of the 4th Battalion formed portion of an army under General Augustine Prevost in Georgia and South Carolina. The Regiment played a leading part at the brilliant action of Briars Creek (March 3rd, 1779), and also in the subsequent siege of Savannah, where a superior force of French and Americans under Comte d'Estaigne and General Lincoln was successfully held at bay by a very much smaller army under Prevost, and at the final assault was signally defeated with great loss (October the 9th, 1779). An improvised body of Light Dragoons (or Mounted Infantry), organised by Lieut.-Colonel Marc Prevost,* of the 60th, did remarkable service during these operations, and at the victory on the 9th of October lost heavily, but greatly distinguished itself by repulsing the main column of the enemy and capturing the colour of the Carolina Regiment, now in the possession of the Prevost family.

1779, SAVANNAH. AMERICAN WAR.

Upon the termination of the American War of Independence in 1783 the 3rd and 4th Battalions were disbanded for the second time, but were again raised in 1788 and despatched to the West Indies.

The Regiment, for the most part quartered in the WEST INDIES

---

* Lieut.-Colonel Marc Prevost, born 1736, died 1785, youngest brother of General Augustine Prevost—a brilliant and most promising officer, who succombed to the effect of his wounds.

West Indies, took part in the following military operations :—

Capture of the Island of Tobago, a
brilliant feat of arms ...	April 17th,	1783
,, (2nd) of Martinique ...	March	1794
,, Saint Lucia		1794
,, Grande Terre Guadaloupe		1794
,, Saint Vincent		1796
,, Trinidad	Feb.	1797
,, Porto Rico	April	1797

On the 23rd of August, 1797, Field-Marshal H.R.H. Frederick Duke of York* was appointed Colonel-in-Chief of the Regiment, *vice* Lord Amherst deceased.

In December of the same year the famous 5th Battalion was raised at Cowes, Isle of Wight, under Lieutenant-Colonel Baron de Rottenburg,† upon the German model as a Special Corps of Riflemen. Four hundred of Hompesch's Mounted Riflemen—a German Corps raised for service under the British Crown— were drafted into the Battalion, which was armed with rifles and dressed in green with red facings. The second Lieutenant-Colonel was that celebrated Robert Crauford, who afterwards made his name so famous in the Peninsular War as the honoured leader of the Light Division. Thus, by the addition of the 5th Battalion to the Regiment as Riflemen in 1797, the gradual evolution of the 60th Royal Americans into The King's Royal Rifle Corps was auspiciously begun.

The system of organisation, drill, and tactics for Light Troops introduced into the Regiment by Baron de Rottenburg, was embodied in a Manual for Riflemen and Light Infantry. This volume ‡ was published

---

* Frederick, Duke of York, was the second son of George III, and brother of George IV and William IV.

† Afterwards Lieutenant-General. Born 1760, died 1832. He commanded the 5th Battalion, 1797–1808. He afterwards served as Major-General commanding in Lower Canada, 1810–1815, during the American War, 1812–13.

‡ *Regulations for the Exercise of Riflemen and Light Infantry and Instructions for their conduct in the Field*, with diagrams, published with a Memo, dated Horse Guards, August 1st, 1798. Copies of the editions 1808 and 1812 will be found in the Library, Royal United Service Institution, Whitehall.

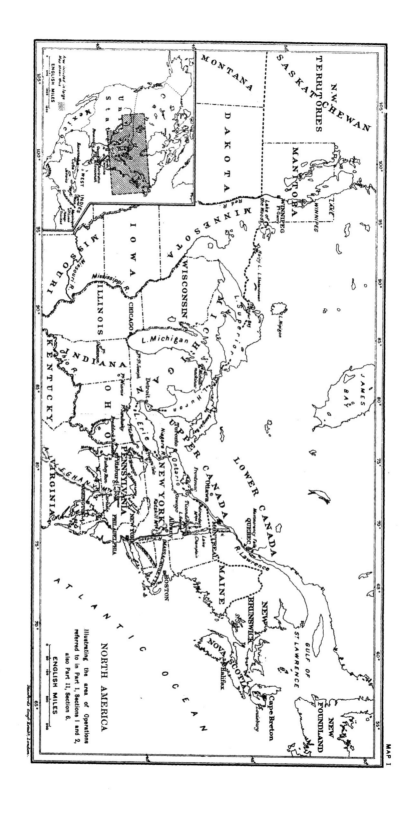

NORTH AMERICA

Illustrating the area of Operations
referred to in Part I, Sections 1 and 2,
also Part II, Section 6.

ENGLISH MILES

MAP I

in August, 1798, with a preface signed by the Adjutant General, and especially commended to the Army by the Commander-in-Chief as a text book on the subject.

In 1799 a 6th Battalion was added to the Regiment, so that the close of the eighteenth century saw the Regiment composed of six battalions.

III.

1808–1824.—PENINSULAR WAR. 60TH THE ROYAL AMERICAN REGIMENT BECOMES 60TH THE DUKE OF YORK'S OWN RIFLE CORPS.

In 1808 Great Britain determined to take the offensive against France, and, by occupying Portugal, endeavour to drive Napoleon and the French from the Peninsula of Spain and Portugal.

Thus began the Peninsular War, so full of glorious memories for the British Army. The 5th Battalion, under the command of Major Davy,* formed part of the force despatched under *Sir Arthur Wellesley* to Portugal, and in conjunction with the 2nd Battalion of the 95th† opened the campaign at Obidos on the 15th of August; and two days later took part in the fight of ROLEIA. The services of the Battalion as Light Troops or Riflemen were valued so highly by the Commander of the forces, and so important was their example, that in a very complimentary order he directed its distribution by companies among the several brigades of the army. Thus it came to be engaged in nearly all the great battles throughout the war, starting brilliantly with the battle of VIMIERA,‡ where a signal victory was gained over the French under General Junot.

Aug. 17th, 1808 ROLEIA.

Aug. 21st, 1808, VIMIERA.

---

* Afterwards General Sir William Gabriel Davy, C.B., K.C.H., Colonel Commandant, 6oth Rifles, 1842–1856. He succeeded Baron de Rottenburg in command of the 5th Battalion in 1808.

† Formed in 1800, and now The Rifle Brigade.

‡ The Battalion was especially mentioned in Wellesley's despatch.

1809.

Wellesley was shortly afterwards superseded by Sir Harry Burrard* and *Sir Hew Dalrymple*, who ended the campaign by the Convention of Cintra, under the terms of which the French evacuated Portugal.

The three commanders were then ordered home, and Sir John Moore† assumed charge of the troops. *Sir David Baird* landed at Corunna with reinforcements, including the 2nd Battalion, and on the 20th of December he joined Moore near Mayorga. By the masterly dispositions of Napoleon himself, an overwhelming force of French was concentrated under Soult, and this forced

ı. 16th, 1809,
RUNNA.

the British to retire on Corunna. Soult, following in pursuit, attacked them in the act of embarking, but met with a crushing defeat. The British, however, paid a high price for their victory: *Baird* was severely wounded, and the gallant Sir John Moore was killed— his death being a heavy loss to the British Army. At this juncture General Hope‡ took over the command and completed the embarkation of the troops. The Regiment, having been allotted to the defence of the town of Corunna, was not actually engaged in the battle.

In 1809 *Wellesley*, for the second time, landed in Portugal and assumed command. After some delay, on May the 12th he forced the passage of the Douro in the face of a large army under Soult, a most brilliant feat of arms. On the 27th and 28th of July he attacked the French and Marshals Jourdan and Victor, under King Joseph, and thereupon ensued the great British

ly 27th and 28th,
1809,
.LAVERA.

victory of TALAVERA. " Upon this occasion," wrote *Sir Arthur Wellesley* in his despatch, " the steadiness and discipline of the 5th Battalion, 60th Regiment, were conspicuous."

* Formerly a Captain in the 60th.

† Formerly Major in the 4th Battalion 60th.

‡ Afterwards General the Earl of Hopetoun, G.C.B., Colonel-Commandant 6th Battalion 60th

On September the 27th, 1810, the British Commander, *Sir Arthur Wellesley*, recently created *Lord Wellington*, signally defeated the French under Massena at the battle of BUSACO; the conduct of the 60th (at this time commanded by Colonel Williams*), being specially noted by *General Picton*.

Yielding to superior numbers and to stress of circumstances, *Wellington* retreated, and, falling back upon the famous lines of Torres Vedras, was closely followed by the French, who, on being stopped by the fortifications and unable to procure supplies, were soon forced in turn to retreat.

In March, 1811, the British again advanced, driving Ney from Pombal and Redinha, and Massena from Casal Nova and Sabugal. While following up his successes, *Wellington* was attacked by Massena at FUENTES D'ONOR, on the 3rd of May, and again on the 5th, but he held his ground in spite of severe fighting. In the meanwhile Marshal Beresford,† who had four companies of the 60th with his division, had in April taken Olivenza, and on the 16th of May had defeated Soult at ALBUHERA; and the campaign of 1811 was brought to a close by the brilliant action of Arroyo dos Molinos by *General Hill* on October the 28th, 1811, when the Regiment specially distinguished itself.

The next year, 1812, opened with the siege, assault, and capture of CIUDAD RODRIGO, and immediately afterwards ensued the successful siege of BADAJOS. Sending *Hill* to destroy the bridge of Almarez, *Wellington* proceeded northwards, and on the 22nd of July defeated Marmont at the battle of SALAMANCA, the crowning feat of a long series of brilliant manœuvres. The English General thereupon marched towards

1810—1812.

Sept. 27th, 181⟨ ⟩
BUSACO

May 3rd and ⟨ ⟩
1811,
FUENTES
D'ONOR.

May 16th, 181⟨ ⟩
ALBUHERA.

1812,
CIUDAD
RODRIG⟨ ⟩
BADAJOS.

July 22nd, 18⟨ ⟩
SALAMANC⟨ ⟩

* Afterwards Major-General Sir William Williams, K.C.B., K.T.S., died 1832.

† Afterwards General Viscount Beresford, G.C.B., G.C.H., Colonel-in-Chief of the 60th Rifles, 1852-54.

Madrid, and, driving King Joseph before him, entered the capital in triumph on the 12th of August. But the French were so strongly reinforced that the British troops were obliged to retire for the winter to Portugal.

In May, 1813, the Army finally quitted Portugal, and again advancing drove the French northwards by brilliant strategy. On the 21st of June *Wellington* gained a splendid victory over King Joseph at

June 21st, 1813, VITTORIA. VITTORIA, capturing 150 guns and his whole transport. The companies of the Regiment with *Picton* and the 3rd Division played an especially brilliant part. Ignominiously driven from Spain the French Army rallied on the Bidassoa, where Soult assumed command, having been despatched by Napoleon to supersede his brother King Joseph and Marshal Jourdan. He immediately attacked the English, but was defeated with

July 24th to Aug. 2nd, 1813, PYRENEES. great slaughter at the battle of the PYRENEES, which lasted eight days, July the 24th to August the 2nd. The 5th Battalion was at this time commanded by Major Fitzgerald.* *Wellington*, then advancing into France, forced the passage of the Bidassoa on October the 7th, and defeated the French at the battle

Nov. 10th, 1813, NIVELLE. of NIVELLE, terminating the campaign by a victory

Dec. 9th to 13th, NIVE. on the NIVE after a battle lasting five days.

In February, 1814, occurred one of the most brilliant manœuvres of the war—the famous passage of the Adour, which was forced in the teeth of a Division of the French Army, the company of the 60th leading the advance of the Guards' Brigade, to which it was attached. On the 27th of the same month Soult was

Feb. 27th, 1814, ORTHES. again totally defeated at ORTHES.

April 10th, 1814, TOULOUSE. *Wellington*, following up this victory, advanced on Toulouse, where, on the 10th of April, the British

---

* Afterwards Field-Marshal Sir John Foster Fitzgerald, G.C.B. Born 1786, died 1877, aged 91.

troops won the last of the fourteen great battles fought in the Peninsular War, in twelve of which the Regiment had taken a glorious part. The repulse of a sortie from Bayonne was the final episode of this memorable war.

Thus closes a momentous record of gallant achievements of the Regiment. Among the officers of the 5th Battalion who distinguished themselves during the Peninsular War, besides those already mentioned, were Major Woodgate,* Lieutenant-Colonel Galiffe,† Captain Schoedde,‡ and Captain de Blacquière.

To continue the history of the other Battalions of the Regiment at this period, the 2nd Battalion, in January, 1809, after Corunna, had returned to the Channel Islands, and thence to the West Indies. The 1st Battalion, which had previously always been quartered in America, was in 1810, together with the 4th Battalion, brought to England, whence it shortly afterwards proceeded to the Cape of Good Hope, and the 4th Battalion was sent to Dominica.

A 7th and 8th Battalion were added in 1813, the former raised at Gibraltar and the latter at Lisbon. Both battalions were dressed in green, which colour at the end of 1815 was adopted for the whole Regiment.

At the conclusion of the war with France the Regiment was reduced to two battalions, of which the 1st was called "The Rifles," and the 2nd "The Light Infantry" Battalion. In 1824 the 2nd Battalion became also a Rifle Battalion, and the Regiment dropping its old title of "Royal Americans" was granted by George IV the name of "The Duke of York's Own Rifle Corps," dated June 4th.

* Afterwards Colonel and C.B., died 1861.
† Afterwards Colonel and C.B., died 1848.
‡ Afterwards Lieut.-General Sir James Holmes Schoedde, K.C.B., who received thirteen clasps with his war medal. Born 1786, died 1861.
  Major-Generals Sir Henry Clinton, Sir George Murray, and Sir James Kampt, Colonels Commandant of the Regiment, also served with distinction.

PART II.—1825—1870.

IV.

1825–1856.—Sikh War—South Africa.

1830,
60th THE DUKE
)F YORK'S OWN
RIFLE CORPS
becomes
60th THE KING'S
ROYAL RIFLE
CORPS.

In 1827 took place the death of Field-Marshal H.R.H. the Duke of York,* who had been Colonel-in-Chief for thirty years, and had given his name to the Regiment. He was succeeded by his brother, Field-Marshal H.R.H. Adolphus, Duke of Cambridge.† In 1830 the title of the Regiment, by order of William IV, was again changed to The King's Royal Rifle Corps.

A long peace followed the great wars of the Napoleonic period, and from Toulouse in 1814 until the Sikh War in 1848 the Regiment was not engaged on active service. But from 1848 onwards the British Army entered upon a famous series of campaigns, in nearly all of which the Regiment has taken a memorable share. Its success may be said to be largely due to the excellence and the example of the 1st Battalion, which—directly inheriting the Peninsular honours and traditions of the 5th Battalion as Riflemen—had maintained, in spite of the long peace, its reputation for smartness, discipline, and warlike efficiency.

Fortunate at this period in many officers of great experience, the Regiment owed much to Lieutenant-Colonel the Hon. Henry Richard Molyneux,‡ who commanded the 1st Battalion (then quartered in the

---

* His Royal Highness's sword and belts were presented to the officers of the 1st Battalion by H.M. King George IV, and are now in the Officers' Mess.

† The seventh son of George III and the Father of the late Field-Marshal H.R.H. George Duke of Cambridge, Colonel-in-Chief, 1869–1904.

‡ 3rd son of 2nd Earl of Sefton. Born 27th August, 1800; died 1841.

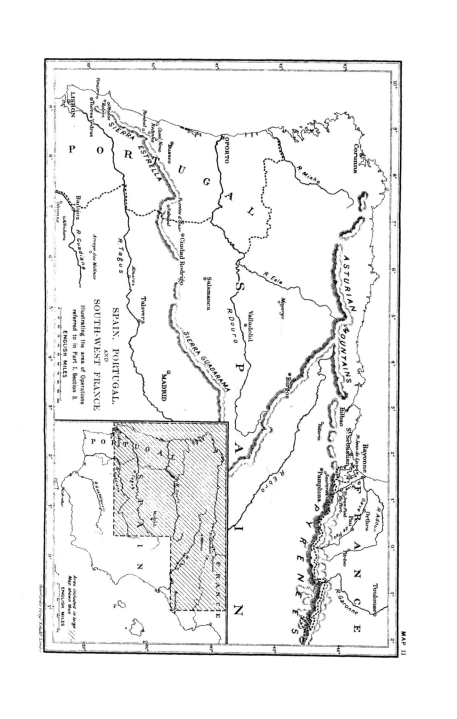

SPAIN, PORTUGAL,
AND
SOUTH-WEST FRANCE.

Illustrating the area of Operations
referred to in Part I, Section 3.

ENGLISH MILES

MAP II

Mediterranean) from 1836 until his untimely death in 1841. The high efficiency of the Battalion and its strong *esprit de corps* when it sailed for India in 1845, under his successor Lieutenant-Colonel the Hon. Henry Dundas,* were largely due to his strong personality and to his powers of organisation. Dundas commanded the Battalion from 1845 to 1854 with conspicuous success. In the Sikh War, both as Colonel and as Brigadier-General, he showed the highest qualities of leadership and courage, and throughout the nine years of his command the Battalion held a foremost place in the British Army in India.

1842—1850.

It was thus under these favourable circumstances that the Regiment began its career in the East, and under Dundas played a prominent part in the Sikh War. Employed in covering the advance, it rendered conspicuous service at the storming of the city of MOOLTAN. " Nothing could exceed the gallantry and discipline of the 60th Royal Rifles " are the words of the *Gazette*, 7th of March, 1849.

1848—49, PUNJAUB.

Jan. 22nd, 1849, MOOLTAN.

Subsequently, by forced marches, the Battalion joined the army under Lord Gough† in time to share in the final battle of GOOJERAT, a victory over a combined force of 60,000 Sikhs and Afghans. The result of this triumph of British arms was the annexation of the Punjaub, and the retreat of the Ameer Dost Mahomed Khan with the Afghan army beyond the Khyber Pass.

Feb. 21st, 1849, GOOJERAT.

Upon the 8th of July, 1850, H.R.H. Adolphus Duke of Cambridge died, and was succeeded as Colonel-in-Chief by Field-Marshal H.R.H. Prince Albert, Consort of Her late Majesty Queen Victoria.

---

* Afterwards General Viscount Melville, G.C.B., Colonel Commandant 1864-1875.

† Afterwards Field-Marshal Viscount Gough, K.P., G.C.B., Colonel-in-Chief 1854-1869.

In 1851 the 2nd Battalion, which had been on home service since 1847, embarked for South Africa, and was employed in the Kaffir War during that and the two following years. It took part under Lieut.-Colonel Nesbitt in many actions with the enemy, including the passage of the Great Kei, the operations for clearing the Water Kloof, and the attack on the Iron Mountain.

A detachment of the 2nd Battalion (forty-one all ranks, with seven women and thirteen children) formed a portion of the troops on board the ill-fated
troopship *Birkenhead*, which, on the night of February the 26th, 1852, was wrecked on the South African coast under conditions which evoked from the troops on board a memorable display of steady discipline and serene courage in the face of danger. The men fell in and stood calmly on parade awaiting death while the ship was sinking " without a cry or murmur among them." The whole ship's company with few exceptions perished.

On September the 23rd, 1852, General Viscount Beresford became Colonel-in-Chief, *vice* H.R.H. Prince Albert, and was upon his death on the 28th of January, 1854, succeeded by Field-Marshal Viscount Gough.

In 1855 and 1857 the 3rd and 4th Battalions were raised at Dublin and at Winchester respectively. Thus in 1857 the Regiment again consisted of four Battalions.

V.

1857–1860.—DELHI. ROHILKUND. PEKIN.

The outbreak of the Great Mutiny of the Native Army in India began on the 10th of May, 1857, at Meerut, where the 1st Battalion was at that time quartered under the command of Lieut.-Colonel John

Jones.* The Battalion at the moment was mustering for evening church parade. On hearing the news it immediately fell in, and Captain Muter,† the senior officer present, with great promptitude instantly despatched a company to secure the Treasury. The Battalion thereupon marched towards the city, when being joined by the 6th Carabiniers and a Battery of Horse Artillery (all the European troops available), it proceeded to occupy the lines of the Native troops, thus effectually preventing the mutineers from establishing themselves in the city, so that they were forced forthwith to retreat towards Delhi. The story is told that while hurrying to the native lines the Battalion came upon the body of a lady lying dead and mutilated by the roadside. This lady was well known both to the officers and men for her devotion and care for the women and children of the Battalion, and the men as they passed— exasperated at the sight—raised their rifles in the air and swore to avenge her death. It is not too much to say that the Battalion, and their leader known later as " Jones the Avenger," made good their oath.

Marching in pursuit, under *Brigadier Archdale Wilson*, the Meerut troops fought two successful actions upon the Hindun River, in which the 1st Battalion took a prominent part, and on the 7th of June it joined the army under *Major-General Sir Henry Barnard* at Alighur.

At one o'clock on the following morning the whole of *Barnard's* force moved against Delhi. On reaching Badlee-ke-Serai it was found that the mutineers were strongly posted in an entrenched position along the ridge from the flagstaff to Hindoo Rao's house, overlooking the cantonments and city, but after a sharp engage-

---

* Afterwards Major-General Sir John Jones, K.C.B.

† Colonel Dunbar Douglas Muter, who greatly distinguished himself, obtaining two brevets during the siege and subsequent operations. He was afterwards a Military Knight of Windsor ; and died in 1909.

ment of about three quarters of an hour the ridge was cleared of the enemy and occupied by our troops. Thus began the famous siege of DELHI—a period full of glorious memories to all Sixtieth Riflemen. From then on to the final assault on the city (June the 8th to September the 20th) the Battalion was constantly employed either as outposts near Hindoo Rao's house, or with the various columns which were sent forward to drive the mutineers back into the city, when, emboldened by the strength of overwhelming numbers, they made repeated assaults upon our position on the ridge. It is recorded that the Regiment was during this period engaged in twenty-four separate actions.

On the morning of September the 14th, after six days of bombardment, two breaches were considered practicable in the walls of the city, one in the curtain to the right of the Cashmere Gate, the other to the left of the water bastion. The assault was delivered at three points, namely upon the two breaches and the Cashmere Gate, while a fourth column followed as reserve. The whole of the Battalion was split up in skirmishing order to cover the advance of the assaulting columns, and in this appropriate and congenial duty they greatly distinguished themselves.

The assaults were successful, and after an heroic struggle the city was partially occupied by night-fall. But it was not until September the 20th that the place and its defences were completely in the hands of our troops, and then only after continuous and desperate hand to hand fighting in the streets. Nothing could exceed the determined valour of the Regiment, and every Rifleman will remember with justifiable pride and pleasure that, having joined the army before Delhi, its services were officially pronounced to be " pre-eminent in the memorable siege and capture."*

* Governor-General's despatch. *London Gazette*, May 18th, 1860, upon the departure of the Regiment from India.

"All behaved nobly," writes Lord Canning, the Governor-General of India in his final despatch upon the siege and capture of Delhi (dated November the 9th, 1857), "but I may be permitted to allude "somewhat to those Corps most constantly engaged "from the beginning, the 60th Rifles, the Sirmoor "Battalion,* and the Guides. Probably not one day "throughout the siege passed without a casualty in "one of these Corps; placed in the very front of our "position, they were ever under fire. Their courage, "their high qualifications as skirmishers, their cheer- "fulness, their steadiness were beyond commendation. "Their losses in action show the nature of the service. "The Rifles commenced with 440 of all ranks; a few "days before the storm they received a reinforcement "of nearly 200 men; their total casualties were 389."

We may conclude this page of the Regiment's history by citing the judgment of the General under whom they served, who described the Battalion as "a glorious example both in its daring gallantry and "its perfect discipline."†

In the following year the 1st Battalion formed part of the Roorkee Field Force under Jones, now promoted Brigadier-General, which operated against the rebels from the 11th of April until the 24th of May, 1858.

During this short campaign Jones' force swept through the whole Province of Rohilkund from north to south; fought one battle (Nugeenah, 21st of April); defeated the enemy in three actions (Bagawalla, 17th of April, Dojura, and Barreilly, 3rd of May); assaulted and captured one city (Bareilly, 6th of May); and relieved two others (Moradabad, 18th of April, and

---

* Now the 2nd King Edward's Own Gurkha Rifles (the Sirmoor Rifles). It is stated of this gallant Regiment that, when asked what reward they would like, they begged for and were granted the red facings of the 60th to be added to their Rifle uniform.

† Despatch, General Sir Archdale Wilson, 22nd September, 1857.

Shahjehanpore, 11th of May); destroyed two forts (Bunnai, 24th of May, and Mahomdee, 25th of May); and took thirty-seven guns. It was said of the gallant Jones that " he never assaulted a position that he did " not take, nor attacked a gun that he did not capture."

The 1st Battalion again took part in operations in Oudh, under Brigadier *Sir Thomas Seaton* and *Brigadier Colin Troup*, from the 8th of October until the 31st of December, 1858. Four successful actions were fought with the rebels (Bunkagaon, 8th of October; Pusgaon, 19th of October; Rissoolpur, 25th of October; and Baragoan, 23rd of November); and the Fort of Mittowlis captured (10th of November); thence the Battalion formed part of a flying column, which cleared the rebels out of the Khyreeghur jungles.

A wing of the 2nd Battalion, which had been ordered from the Cape, also took part in the final stages of the operations against the mutineers.

In March, 1860, the 1st Battalion embarked for England, and in a General Order Lord Canning, Governor-General of India, bore further testimony to the services of the Battalion in eloquent and unprecedented terms, concluding with the following memorable tribute:

" It is not more by the valour of its officers and " men, conspicuous as that has been on every occasion, " than by the discipline and excellent conduct of all ranks " during the whole of their service in India, that this Regi- " ment has distinguished itself. The Governor-General " tenders to the Battalion his warmest acknowledgments " for the high example it has set in every respect to the troops " with which it has been associated in quarters as well as " in the field; and he assures its officers and men that " the estimation in which their services are held by " the Government of India confirms to the full the respect " and admiration with which they are universally regarded."*

* *London Gazette*, May 18th, 1860.

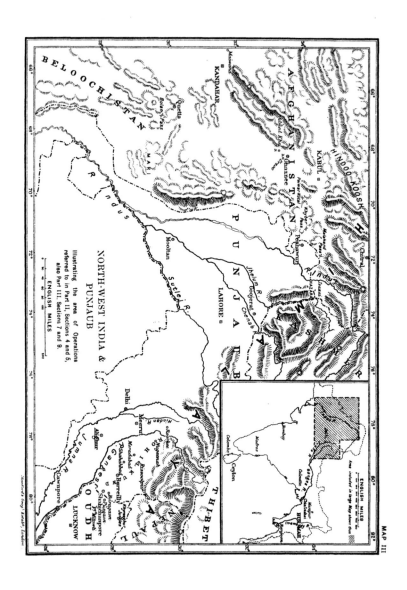

NORTH-WEST INDIA &
PUNJAUB

Illustrating the area of Operations
referred to in Part II, Sections 4 and 5,
also Part III, Sections 7 and 9.

ENGLISH MILES

BELOOCHISTAN

AFGHANISTAN

HINDOO-KOOSH

KANDAHAR

Quetta

Bolan Pass

KABUL

PUNJAUB

LAHORE

Mooltan

Peshawur

Khyber Pass

Cabul R.

Jhelum R.

Chenab R.

Sutlej R.

Indus

Indus

Delhi

Meerut

Agra

Cawnpore

LUCKNOW

OUDH

THIBET

MAP III

ENGLISH MILES

Area included in large Map above that

Stanford's Geog.l Estab.t London

The splendid services rendered by the Regiment in the period in its history above briefly recorded may perhaps be equalled, but can hardly be surpassed by future generations of Riflemen. The good conduct, sound discipline, and unflinching courage of the 1st Battalion during its service in India (1845–1860) will always be regarded by the Regiment as marking a Golden Age in its history and a landmark in its traditions.

1860–1861.

On the 28th of February, 1860, the 2nd Battalion, under Lieutenant-Colonel Palmer,* embarked at Calcutta to join the Franco-British Expedition to China under *General Sir Hope Grant.* Six months later the Battalion took a vigorous part in the assault and capture of the TAKU FORTS on the Peiho River (August the 21st), and thence marched to and occupied PEKIN on the 13th of September.

Aug. 21st, 1860.
TAKU FORTS.

PEKIN.

In September, 1861, the Battalion returned to England.

VI.

1861–1870.—NORTH AMERICA. RED RIVER.

In 1861 the 4th Battalion was hurriedly despatched to Canada at the time of the Trent affair, when war with the Northern States of America seemed imminent, and Fenian raids were threatened. This Battalion— commanded for fourteen years (1860–1873) by Lieutenant-Colonel Hawley,† an officer of commanding personality and ability—achieved at this period

1861,
TRENT AFFAI

---

* Afterwards Colonel and C. B.

† Afterwards Lieut.-General Hawley, C.B., Colonel Commandant, 1890-98, *vide* Biographical Sketch, *Regimental Chronicle*, 1909.

and later the highest reputation for its system of light drill and of organisation then far in advance of the age, a system which has gradually been adopted by the whole Army. The Regiment, both individually and collectively, is deeply indebted to Hawley. Sir Redvers Buller * and Lord Grenfell † owed their early training to his tuition; and there are few Riflemen of our generation who have achieved distinction who do not directly or indirectly owe their success to his inspiration and teaching, and his influence is still generally acknowledged in the Regiment to-day.

In 1869 the 4th Battalion returned to England, and was quartered at Aldershot, where its high state of efficiency was universally acknowledged.

Upon the death of Lord Gough, on the 3rd of March, 1869, Field-Marshal H.R.H. George Duke of Cambridge,‡ the Commander-in-Chief of the British Army, was appointed Colonel-in-Chief.

In 1867 the 1st Battalion, under Lieutenant-Colonel Feilden,§ was moved from the Mediterranean to Canada, and on the outbreak of Riel's Rebellion in 1870 was selected by *Colonel Wolseley*‖ to take part in the Red River Expedition. The force, numbering 1200, consisted of two guns, R.A., the 1st Battalion 60th Rifles, and two specially raised battalions of Canadian Militia. After a journey of 600 miles by land and lake, it

---

* Afterwards General Right Hon. Sir Redvers Buller, P.C., V.C., G.C.B., G.C.M.G., Colonel Commandant, 1895–1908. Born December 7th 1839, died June 2nd, 1908. His qualities as a distinguished soldier are well summed up by the inscription upon his Memorial Tomb recently erected in Winchester Cathedral, "A Great Leader—Beloved by his Men." *Vide* Biographical Sketch, *Regimental Chronicle*, 1908, p. 157.

† Now Field-Marshal Right Hon. F. W. Lord Grenfell, P.C., G.C.B., G.C.M.G., Colonel Commandant, 1898. Born April 29th, 1841.

‡ H.R.H. George Duke of Cambridge died upon the 17th March, 1904, and was succeeded as Colonel-in-Chief by General H.R.H. the Prince of Wales, now His Majesty George V.

§ Afterwards Lieut.-General Feilden, C.M.G., died 1895.

‖ Now Field-Marshal Viscount Wolseley, K.P., etc.

reached Thunder Bay, on Lake Superior. Leaving Lake Shebandowah, fifty miles from Lake Superior, on the 16th of July, the Expedition then traversed in boats 600 miles of a region of rivers, lakes, and forest, practically unexplored and trackless, and after six weeks of incessant toil, on the 24th of August reached Fort Garry (now the city of Winnipeg), the headquarters of the rebel forces under Louis Riel. *Wolseley*, by a brilliant *coup de main*, pushed on with the 1st Battalion in fifty boats, and took Riel and his followers completely by surprise. Hurriedly the insurgent leader abandoned Fort Garry, and the rebellion collapsed.

The direct effect of this achievement, in which the Regiment was fortunate enough to take so prominent and decisive a share, has been the unification of the Dominion of Canada and the opening up to a great and prosperous future of the whole wide region of the great North-west, destined to become one of the most populous and most important portions of the Empire.

Thus for a second time has the 1st Battalion of the Regiment been privileged to play a direct and almost single-handed part in the addition of vast regions to the British Crown in North America: first, in 1758–1764, under Bouquet, in conquering those territories west of the Alleghany Mountains, now some of the most prosperous States of the American Union; and, second, in 1870, under *Wolseley*, in crushing a rebellion, the overthrow of which has enabled the prairies of the North-west Territories of Canada to be welded into what are now among the most flourishing Provinces of the Dominion.

PART   III.—1871—1902.

VII.

1871–1881.—India. Afghan War. South Africa. Zulu War. First Boer War.

The overwhelming defeat of the French Armies by the German troops in the momentous war of 1870–71 brought about vast changes in military Europe. A system of compulsory service on the German model was introduced by all the great nations of Europe— Great Britain excepted—and German drill, German style of uniform, and German methods were generally adopted.

In England a strong wave of pro-German feeling swept over the British Army, and military critics advocated the methodical system of the German Army with its stern unbending discipline and exacting method of machine-like *collectivism*, to the destruction of the elasticity and rapidity of movement, with the self-reliance and initiative which makes for *individualism*.

The spirit of the 60th stood out, and did much to counteract this tendency, and to bring about the re-action.

In the autumn of 1878 the 2nd Battalion, commanded in the absence of Lieutenant-Colonel J. J. Collins by Major Cromer Ashburnham, was quartered at Meerut, and formed part of the 1st Brigade, 1st Division, under *Lieutenant-General Sir Donald Stewart*, which, upon the outbreak of the Afghan War, was directed upon Kandahar.

After a trying march of 440 miles (one day thirty miles across the desert without a man falling out)

Kandahar was occupied without resistance on the 8th of January, 1879.

In the following September there was a rising of the Afghans at Kabul, and the British envoy and his escort were massacred. An advance upon Kabul, the necessary retort to such an outrage, was accordingly made by two columns, and after severe fighting Kabul was occupied by *Lieut.-General Sir Frederick Roberts.**

On the 27th of March, 1880, *Sir Donald Stewart's* Division of 7250 men was directed to leave Kandahar and march upon Kabul. On the 19th of April the Afghan Army attacked the column on the march at AHMAD KHEL, when, concealed in the khors and gorges of the hills, a large body of Ghazies charged boldly upon the flank of the first line. Carrying all before them, the issue for a time seemed doubtful, but the stubborn courage of the British column won the day, and the formidable Ghazies after suffering great loss, were totally defeated. The 2nd Battalion then commanded by Collins, had the ill-fortune to be taking its turn of rear and flank guard on this particular day, but, on hearing the firing, at once hurried to the scene in time to bear a leading part in retrieving the critical situation and aid in turning what at the onset threatened to be a serious reverse into a decisive victory. G Company, however, under Lieut. Davidson,† allotted to the permanent duty of escort to *Sir Donald Stewart*, played a prominent part in meeting the first sudden onslaught of the Ghazies, and did much to stem the rush which at the moment seemed likely to be overwhelming. Continuing the march, the Battalion was present at the surrender of Ghuznee, and at the fight

---

* Now Field-Marshal Earl Roberts, K.G., V.C., etc., whose only son, Lieut. the Hon. Frederick Roberts, V.C., was killed at the battle of Colenso, December 15th, 1899, when an officer of the Regiment, and serving as A.D.C. to Sir Redvers Buller.

† Now Colonel Sir Arthur Davidson, K.C.B., K.C.V.O., Equerry to H.M. Queen Alexandra.

of Urzoo on the 23rd of April when the Afghans were again defeated. The column finally reached Kabul on the 28th of the same month, thus accomplishing a notable march. It had covered 320 miles in thirty-five days over a hostile, difficult, and almost unknown country, fought two general actions, and captured a fortress.

In July Ayub Khan defeated a British force at Maiwand, and besieged *General Primrose* in Kandahar. The Battalion, already distinguished for its marching powers and steady discipline, was selected to form part of the Relief Force of 10,000 men, which left Kabul under *Sir Frederick Roberts* on the 9th of August, and reached Kandahar on the 31st. This march—by the same route as that of *Sir Donald Stewart*, but at the hottest time of the year—was effected in twenty-four days, inclusive of halts, giving an average of 13·3 miles per diem, or of 14·5 for the days of actual marching.

On the 21st of August *Sir Frederick Roberts* had notified in the orders of the day that the city of Kandahar was completely invested, characteristically adding that he " hoped Ayub Khan would remain there." This wish was duly realised, for the Afghan leader was found in position for battle, and on the following day, September the 1st, he was attacked in front and flank, and completely routed; the whole of his guns and camp (which had been left standing) were captured by the victorious troops.

On the 8th of September the 2nd Battalion left Kandahar to take part in the Mari Expedition, which lasted for two months and entailed much hard marching; there was not, however, any fighting.

On the termination of the campaign the Commander-in-Chief in India published the following General Order:

" The 2nd Battalion 60th Rifles has throughout the war " maintained its high reputation for efficiency. In the

" march from Kandahar to Kabul, at Ahmad Khel, in
" the memorable march from Kabul to Kandahar, and the
" subsequent expedition to the Mari country, the 60th
" Rifles were remarkable for their discipline and marching
" powers. In the operations above described the Regiment
" marched 1000 miles in 100 days. No light feat anywhere,
" but in such a country as Afghanistan it is one well worthy
" of record in the annals of the British Army."

On the 8th of September Lieutenant-Colonel J. J.
Collins, who had commanded the Battalion throughout
the campaign, succumbed to fever while on his way
to India on sick leave.

In addition to the war medal, a special bronze star
was given for the march from Kabul to Kandahar.
It is worthy of note that khaki was worn, and that this
was the first campaign in which the Regiment, since
it had become Rifles, had fought in any colour but
green.

Special reference must here be made to the 3rd
Battalion, whose good fortune led it to take part in
no less than four campaigns in six years, and thus to
justify a claim to being called " the fighting Battalion "
Raised in 1855 in Ireland, this Battalion had been
moved to Madras at the close of the Mutiny in 1857,
to Burmah in 1862, back to Madras in 1865, and to
Aden in 1871, and thence to England in 1872. It
had not unnaturally suffered much disadvantage from
its long exile of fifteen years in the East, unrelieved
by the experience of active service. It was, therefore,
in a condition particularly to profit by the example
of Hawley and the 4th Battalion, which had begun
to be generally felt, and there can be no doubt
that it derived at this period an immense benefit in
efficiency and interior economy, not only from the
influence of Hawley and his system, but also from
the traditions and example of the 1st Battalion. Its

new commanding officer, Pemberton,* and its second in command, Northey,† had both been trained under Hawley, and many of its captains and junior officers, as well as N.C.O.'s, had been promoted or transferred from the 1st and 4th Battalions to the 3rd on its return from India. These officers and men brought with them into the Battalion the vigorous spirit of the Regiment, its flexible drill and tactics, its ideals of rapidity and elasticity of movement, rendered possible by the most careful attention to detail; its extreme steadiness in close formations; and, above all, that assiduous care for the comfort and well-being of the rank and file, which is its great feature. In consequence, the rapidity and smartness of manœuvre, the strong self-reliance and individuality of the Riflemen, and the excellent feeling existing between officers and men were conspicuously the attributes of the rejuvenated 3rd Battalion. The Battalion, therefore, not only won for itself a great reputation as a fighting unit, but conveyed later the same spirit to the Mounted Infantry, for the inception and success of which its officers and Riflemen were largely responsible.

Having been quartered for several years at Aldershot, where it gained much credit, the Battalion was at Colchester in January, 1879, when it received sudden orders to embark for South Africa in consequence of the defeat of *Lord Chelmsford's* troops by Cetewayo, the Zulu King, at the battle of Insandlwana. It landed at Durban, commanded by Lieutenant-Colonel Leigh-Pemberton, and marched direct to the Tugela, where, under *Lord Chelmsford* himself, it formed part of the column to relieve Fort Pierson. Leaving the Tugela on the 25th of March, it took a distinguished

* Now Major-General Sir Wykeham Leigh-Pemberton, K.C.B., Colonel Commandant, 1906. Born 4th December, 1833.

† Afterwards Lieut.-Colonel Northey, mortally wounded at the Battle of Gingihlovo, Zulu War, April 2nd, 1879.

part in the battle of Gingihlovo on the 2nd of April, when the Zulu impis with a splendid gallantry charged up to the muzzles of the men's rifles, and severely tried the young soldiers of whom the ranks were largely composed. After a short half hour's hard fighting the Zulu army reluctantly withdrew, leaving an immense number of killed and wounded behind them. The casualties were light, but the Battalion sustained a great loss in the death of Major and Brevet-Lieutenant-Colonel Frank Northey, who was mortally wounded early in the action.

In June the Battalion was engaged in the second advance to Ulundi under *Sir Garnet Wolseley*; and in the subsequent pursuit and capture of Cetewayo, which brought the Zulu War to a close, two companies of the Battalion, under Captain Astley Terry,* had a prominent share.

The 3rd Battalion, under Lieutenant-Colonel Cromer Ashburnham,† remained in South Africa, and was quartered at Pietermaritzburg, when in January, 1881, the Boers, under Joubert, invaded Natal. *Major-General Sir George Colley*, the High Commissioner and Commander-in-Chief, having assembled at Newcastle a small force, which included the 3rd Battalion, advanced and attacked the Boers on the 28th in position at Laing's Nek. The Battalion in part covered the left flank, and in part formed a reserve to the assaulting column. The attack was repulsed with heavy loss, and the Battalion covered the retreat, but did not lose many men.

On the 25th of January the 2nd Battalion arrived from India in a state of the highest efficiency after its successful experience in the Afghan War. Landing

---

* Now Major-General.

† Now Major-General Sir Cromer Ashburnham, K.C.B., Colonel Commandant, 1907. Born 13th September, 1831. He succeeded Colonel Leigh-Pemberton, and commanded the 3rd Battalion throughout three campaigns, namely, Boer War, 1881 ; Egypt, 1882 ; Suakim, 1884, with conspicuous success, and was popularly known among his men as the "Lion of the Ingogo."

at Durban, it marched forthwith to join headquarters at Newcastle, where it remained until the armistice in March.

The Boers, as a result of their victory at Laing's Nek, made a desperate effort to sever the communications between *Colley's* force at Mount Prospect, and the advanced base at Newcastle. The General accordingly took prompt steps to avert this catastrophe, and thus it came about that on the 8th of February was fought on the Ingogo Heights an action as glorious as any in the history of the 60th. *Colley*, with two 9-pounder R.A. guns, thirty-eight men of the Mounted Infantry, and five companies of the 3rd Battalion, under Ashburnham, marched early on the 8th from Prospect upon Newcastle, crossed the Ingogo River, and, on ascending the heights beyond, was attacked from all sides shortly before noon. The British position was a plateau covered with short grass, rocks, and boulders; whereas the kloofs and slopes occupied by the Boers were also not only strewn with rocks, but overgrown with long grass, which being three and four feet high afforded excellent cover. The troops, though completely surrounded, maintained the fight for nearly seven hours, until at last, in the gloom of approaching night and a heavy thunderstorm, the fire ceased and the enemy sullenly withdrew.

The Battalion had lost five out of thirteen officers, and 119 out of 295 other ranks; of I Company only one officer and thirteen men were left, but nowhere had the enemy gained ground. The survivors, without food or water, and with ammunition running short, but with courage and discipline still unshaken, then faced the last ordeal of that long day. Little could be done for the wounded, except to collect and leave them with the chaplain, the doctor, and a few other noncombatants; and then, in drenching rain and darkness only broken by flashes of lightning, the few remaining horses were hooked into the guns, and the little force moved silently across the veldt to the river, which was in flood, and had to be forded breast high. So slippery was the ground from the rain that the horses could not draw the guns; this for the last few miles was done by the Riflemen. At 8.30 a.m. the following morning Prospect Camp was reached after a peculiarly strenuous test of the courage and endurance of the troops.

" The conduct of all ranks throughout this trying day was admirable," wrote *Sir George Colley* in his despatch.* " The comparatively young soldiers of the " 60th Rifles behaved with the steadiness and coolness " of veterans. At all times perfectly in hand, they " held or changed their ground as directed without " hurry or confusion; though under heavy fire, them- " selves fired steadily, husbanding their ammunition, " and at the end of the day, with sadly reduced numbers, " formed and moved off the ground with the most " perfect steadiness and order; and, finally, after " eighteen hours of continuous fatigue, readily and " cheerfully attached themselves to the guns, and " dragged them up the long hill from the Ingogo, when " the horses were unable to do so."

On the night of the 26th of February *Sir George Colley* decided to seize Majuba Hill by a night march —a hazardous undertaking which was ably executed. The following day the Boers in three assaulting columns, covered by the rifle fire of their largely superior force, carried the mountain with splendid gallantry, and completely defeated the small British force of 414 soldiers and sailors.

Feb. 27th, 1881, MAJUBA.

Two companies of the 3rd Battalion were posted upon the lower spurs of the mountain, and with a third

* Despatch, Mount Prospect, February 12th, 1881, para. 20.

D

company sent out later with ammunition they covered the retreat, but were only slightly engaged.

The brave and accomplished *Colley*—dauntless to the end—died a soldier's death upon the summit of the mountain, and deplorable indeed was the loss in officers and men of the force engaged. A peace—insisted upon by the British Government—brought this unhappy campaign to a close little to the satisfaction of the troops concerned.

VIII.

1882–1885. EGYPT. TEL EL KEBIR, 1882. EL TEB, TAMAI, 1884.—NILE EXPEDITION, 1884–85— MOUNTED INFANTRY.

The 3rd Battalion, under Colonel Ashburnham, had been moved from South Africa to Malta, when the outbreak of hostilities in Egypt caused it to be despatched with the 38th Regiment to Cyprus and Alexandria in July, 1882.

On the 18th of July, shortly after the bombardment of Alexandria, it landed while the city was still in flames, and formed part of the advanced force under *Major-General Sir Archibald Alison.* A portion of the Battalion took part with the Mounted Infantry, on the 22nd of July, in the first engagement of the campaign at Mallaha Junction, eight miles from Alexandria, and again in the reconnaissance in force on the 5th August near Ramleh.

On August the 18th, upon the arrival of *Sir Garnet Wolseley*, it embarked for Ismailia, and took part in the actions of Tel-el-Mahuta on the 25th, and Kassassin on the 9th of September, when the enemy, about 13,000 strong, was completely defeated.

The Battalion, temporarily commanded by Major

Ogilvy,* formed part of the 4th Brigade under Colonel Ashburnham, which had been organised for the night march of the 12th–13th September and the assault of the lines of Te-el-Kebir at daylight. The Brigade forming the support of the Highland Brigade closed up at the beginning of the battle as day began to dawn, and gave a timely assistance in the assault of the enemy's lines. The Battalion in two lines pressed eagerly forward with its accustomed dash, and entered the Egyptian works at about the centre of the position, where Major Cramer, second in Command, was wounded, and had his horse shot under him. After an ebb and flow of strenuous bayonet fighting the enemy gave way on all sides, and, suffering great losses, were broken and dispersed in headlong flight. Two days later Cairo was captured, and the war ended, upon which the Battalion formed part of the army of occupation.

1882–1884.

Sept. 13th, 1882,
TEL-EL-KEBIR.

In February, 1884, the Battalion, under Ashburnham, was ordered to Suakim, where it served in a Brigade under that distinguished Rifleman, Major-General Sir Redvers Buller,† as part of *General Sir Gerald Graham's* force. On the 29th of February it took part in the defeat of the Dervishes at El Teb, and on the 13th of March it was present at the critical battle of Tamai. The troops were in two squares, one under *Sir Gerald Graham*, commanding the force, the other under Buller. *Graham's* square was broken, and in the confusion some of its men poured a volley into Buller's, causing one face to run in. Sir Redvers at once rode outside the square, and, with great coolness, rallied his men. By restoring the formation he undoubtedly staved off a terrible disaster, for, had the square been really broken, nothing could have saved the army. This action ended the Campaign.

1884,
EL TEB, TAMAI

---

* Afterwards Colonel and C.B.

† Afterwards General Right Hon. Sir Redvers Buller, *vide* p. 40 note.

The history of the 3rd Battalion at this period would not be complete without reference to the introduction of Mounted Infantry into the British Army. It may be fairly said that the creation of Mounted Infantry, the establishment of a recognised system for its training, and the development of its tactics, is largely the work of Officers and Riflemen of the 60th, and in a very special degree of the 3rd Battalion.

The value of Mounted Infantry under modern conditions of war was established by the phenomenal success of the relatively small force of Mounted Infantry in Egypt in 1882. This corps, raised and organised by an officer of the 60th,* owed much of its success to the officers and men drawn from the 3rd Battalion who had similarly served in the Boer war; its high reputation for individual gallantry and initiative was universally acknowledged, and there was no engagement in the war, from the preliminary skirmishes before Alexandria in July, until the capture, by a *coup de main*, of the citadel of Cairo at mid-night of the 14th–15th September, in which the Mounted Infantry did not take a distinguished share.†

At Cairo, early in 1884, the inception and scheme of organisation for the Mounted Camel Regiments was also the work of an officer of the 60th Rifles. The Mounted Infantry Camel Regiment in particular which rendered such distinguished service with the Desert Column, under the late *General Sir Herbert Stewart*, was raised and equipped by the same officer, and was largely composed of officers and men of the 60th. Two out of the four companies were commanded by officers of the 60th (Fetherstonhaugh‡ and Berkeley Pigott,§

* Captain Hutton, now Lieut.-General Sir Edward Hutton, K.C.M.G., C.B. Colonel Commandant, 1908. Born December 6th, 1848.

† *Vide* "Cool Courage," an episode of the Egyptian War, 1882—*Regimental Chronicle*, 1908.

‡ Now Major-General R. S. R. Fetherstonhaugh, C.B.

§ Afterwards Lieutenant-Colonel Berkeley Pigott, C.B., D.S.O., 21st Lancers.

both of whom had served with the 3rd Battalion in South Africa), and six out of the sixteen subaltern company officers were also Riflemen.*

In June, 1886, a comprehensive scheme for raising and training Mounted Infantry in England was first proposed, before a public audience, by an officer of the 60th, under the powerful wing of *Lord Wolseley,* and in November of the same year Mounted Infantry were raised and trained under Captain Lewis Butler at Shorncliffe from detachments of the 2nd Battalion and other regiments, under the effective supervision of *Colonel Sir Baker Russell.*†

When, in 1887, it was subsequently decided to form a regiment of Mounted Infantry for service with the Cavalry Division, composed of detachments from nearly all infantry battalions on home service, the command and organisation was again given to an officer of the 60th, and, out of the eight companies composing the original regiment, the 60th and Rifle Brigade found two, or one-fourth of the whole corps   The Mounted Infantry movement therefore may be said to owe its inception, and in a large measure its success, to the officers of the 60th, and to their riflemen.

The Mounted Infantry system thus begun was largely developed, so that upon the outbreak of the South African war in 1899 there were many thousands of officers and men throughout the infantry of the Army who had been trained as Mounted Infantry. It has been rightly said‡ that the ultimately successful issue of the late campaign was in a great measure due to " the large number of Mounted Infantry officers previously trained, and to the long work of prepara-

---

* W. Pitcairn Campbell, P. S. Marling, A. Miles, R. L. Bower, and two officers of The Rifle Brigade, namely, W. M. Sherston and Hon. H. Hardinge.

† Afterwards General Sir Baker Russell, G.C.B., K.C.M.G., etc., a well-known Cavalry General and leader of men.   Died November, 1911.

‡ " *Times* " *History of the War,* Vol. II, p. 31.

1835—1895.

tion carried on before the war by the Mounted Infantry enthusiasts." If this is so, The King's Royal Rifle Corps may lay a fair claim to a goodly share of such an important result.

IX.

1886–1898.—INDIAN FRONTIER. CHITRAL. MANIPUR. WRECK OF THE " WARREN HASTINGS."

1891,
INDIAN
FRONTIER.

In March, 1891, the 1st Battalion, then recently arrived in India, formed part of the 3rd Brigade, Hazara Field Force, and took part in the operations on the Samana Range, where Colonel Cramer,* commanding the Battalion, was severely wounded; and the command throughout the remainder of the campaign devolved upon Major the Hon. Keith Turnour.† The Battalion also took part in the expedition sent into the Sheikhan country and Khanki Valley, and in the action at Mastaon.

1891,
MANIPUR.

During the same period the 4th Battalion, under command of Lieutenant-Colonel R. Chalmer,‡ formed part of the successful Manipur Expedition in April, and from December in the same year until May, 1892, was continually employed with various columns in Burma and the Chin Lushai country.

1895,
CHITRAL.

In September, 1892, the 1st Battalion took part in the Isazai Expedition. In March, 1895, it again took the field under Lieutenant-Colonel H. B. MacCall, § and formed part of the Chitral Relief Force, serving with the leading brigade under Brigadier-General A. A. Kinloch. ‖ The Battalion highly distinguished itself in the battle of the Malakand

---

* Afterwards C.B.

† Now Lieut.-Colonel the Hon. Keith Turnour-Fetherstonhaugh, of Up Park, Petersfield.   ‡ Afterwards Colonel and C.B.

§ Now Brigadier-General and C.B.   ‖ Now Major-General and C.B.

on the 3rd of April, and again in the action at Khar on the following day, thereby adding CHITRAL to the honours of the Regiment.

At the end of 1896 the 1st Battalion, under command of Lieut.-Colonel M. C. B. Forestier-Walker, left India, and embarked on the Royal Indian Marine Troopship, *Warren Hastings.* Leaving four companies at Cape Town, the headquarters of the battalion and the remaining four companies proceeded to the Mauritius, when the ship steaming at full speed on a very dark night, struck upon the rocks off the Island of Reunion at 2.20 a.m. on the 14th January, 1897, and became a total wreck.*

The troops on board, in addition to the Headquarters and four companies of the Rifles, consisted of four companies of the York and Lancaster Regiment, and a small detachment of the Middlesex Regiment, which, with women and children, numbered in all 995. They " at once fell in on the main deck in perfect order until 4 a.m., when the (Naval) Commander ordered their disembarkation to commence by rope ladders from the bows. . . . . . At 4.20 a.m. the position of the vessel appeared so critical that he at once ordered the disembarkation of the men to cease, and the women, children, and sick to be passed out. This order was promptly carried out; the men clung to the side as they stood (the ship lurching and bumping heavily), and passed out the women and children through; no man murmuring or moving from his post."†

At 4.35 a.m., as the ship was in imminent danger of heeling over and sinking, it became necessary to expedite the landing. Owing to the " remarkable courage and exemplary discipline " displayed, the whole

---

* *Vide Regimental Chronicle,* 1909, p. 60.
† Special Army Order, March 13th, 1897.

ship's company, except two natives, were safely passed on to the rocks and saved. " Lieutenant-Colonel Forestier-Walker,* who was in command, was the last soldier to leave the ship."

" The Commander-in-Chief,"† ends the Special Army Order of March the 13th, 1897, by declaring that he " is proud of the behaviour of the troops during this trying time. He regards it as a good example of the advantages of subordination and strict discipline, for it was by that alone, under God's Providence, that heavy loss of life was prevented."

The Regiment will always cherish the honoured memory of Colonel Forestier-Walker and of their comrades, who were thus given the opportunity of supplying one of the finest examples of high discipline, which the annals of the British Army can show.

X.

1899–1902.—SOUTH AFRICA. TALANA HILL.
DEFENCE OF LADYSMITH. RELIEF OF LADYSMITH.
TRANSVAAL.

Note.— As the following section deals with contemporaneous events and with members of the Regiment still serving, it has been considered advisable to adopt a simple form of record of events by Battalions and units, leaving to a future historian the compilation of a complete narrative.

FIRST BATTALION.

1st BATTALION.   When, on October the 7th, 1899, war was declared by President Kruger and the Boer Government, the 1st Battalion, under the command of Lieutenant-

---

* Promoted Colonel for his conduct, and was selected for Staff employment as Chief Staff Officer in Egypt, where he was accidentally killed upon the 31st July, 1902.

† Field-Marshal Viscount Wolseley.

Colonel Robert Henry Gunning, was at Dundee, Natal, with the exception of G Company, which was at Eshowe in Zululand, and there remained until after the following March.

At Talana Hill (20th of October), the first battle of the war, the Battalion greatly distinguished itself in the attack of the Boer position, and took a leading part in the complete defeat of the enemy.* Lieutenant-Colonel Gunning was killed leading the assault, and out of seventeen officers present, five were killed and eight wounded, together with many N.C.O.'s and Riflemen. Major W. Pitcairn Campbell† thereupon assumed command.

Then came the retreat to Ladysmith by a forced march under peculiarly trying circumstances, and on the 30th October took place the battle of Lombard's Kop, which, indecisive in its effect, led to the investment by the Boer Army. The four months DEFENCE OF LADYSMITH was the result, the chief battle being that of Waggon Hill on January the 6th, 1900.

Up to March, 1900, the Battalion lost eight officers and forty-three men killed, eight officers and 180 men wounded, and eighty-one men who died in hospital.

After the Relief of Ladysmith, on the 3rd of March, the Battalion joined the 8th Brigade, 5th Division, and was with Buller's advance into the Transvaal, taking part in the passage of the Biggarsberg in May, the attacks on Botha's Pass and Alleman's Nek (8th and 11th of June).

In August the Battalion assisted in the capture of Amersfoort and Ermelo, and was present at the battle of Belfast (August the 27th), when the armies under *Roberts* and Buller first joined forces, taking part in the attack on Bergendal.

---

* *Vide Official History of the War*, Vol. I, pp. 131–136.

† Now Major-General, C.B., and lately A.D.C. to the King.

It subsequently assisted in the occupation of Lydenburg (6th of September), and at the fighting in the Mauchberg (9th of September), and at Pilgrim's Rest (27th of September). On October the 16th, 1900, the Battalion returned to Middelburg, where it was continually engaged in minor operations until July, 1901, when it proceeded to Cape Colony. Here it built the seventy miles of blockhouses between De Aar and Orange River, which it occupied till the end of the war in June, 1902.

Second Battalion.

ıd BATTALION. The 2nd Battalion left India, and landed in Natal in October, 1899, under the command of Lieutenant-Colonel G. Grimwood, and proceeded at once to Ladysmith, taking part in the battles of Rietfontein (October the 24th) and Lombard's Kop, in which it fought alongside the 1st Battalion. It served through the DEFENCE OF LADYSMITH, and greatly distinguished itself in the famous fight on Waggon Hill of January the 6th.

Up to the 31st of March the Battalion lost five officers (including two attached) and twenty-six men killed in action, seventy-five men wounded, and 107 who died in hospital.

After the relief it was under the command of Major the Hon. E. J. Montagu-Stuart-Wortley,* and, with the 1st Battalion, formed part of the 8th Brigade, 5th Division until the 1st of August, 1900, when it proceeded to Ceylon in charge of prisoners of war.

Third Battalion.

rd BATTALION. The 3rd Battalion, under the command of Lieut.-Colonel Robert George Buchanan-Riddell, left England

* Now Brigadier-General, C.B., C.M.G., M.V.O., D.S.O.

in November, 1899, with the 4th Light Infantry Brigade, under Major-General the *Hon. N. G. Lyttelton,* and landed at Durban on the 30th. It took part in all the battles for the RELIEF OF LADYSMITH, namely, Colenso (December the 15th), Spion Kop (January the 24th), Vaal Krantz (5th–7th of February), and the fourteen days continuous fighting from the 13th to the 27th of February, including the actions at Cingolo, Monte Christo, Hlangwane, Hart's Hill, and the final battle of Pieter's Hill, on February the 27th, Majuba Day. The Battalion rightly cherishes with pride the names of Spion Kop, Vaal Krantz, and Hart's Hill. At Spion Kop* it captured by a bold and vigorous stroke the famous Twin Peaks single-handed, rightly considered one of the most notable feats of the war. Lieutenant-Colonel Buchanan-Riddell was killed on the summit at the moment of victory while leading his men, and Major R. Bewicke-Copley† thereupon assumed command. At Vaal Krantz, after being engaged for twenty-four hours, the Battalion highly distinguished itself in repulsing the Boer counter-attack.‡ At Hart's Hill four companies were prominent in the desperate struggle during the night of the 22nd–23rd of February, delivering two bayonet charges and losing over a third of their number in killed and wounded.§ Part of the Rifle Reserve Battalion was also engaged in this fight. The Battalion lost during this portion of the campaign three officers and forty-six men killed in action, eleven officers and 195 men wounded, while fifty-nine men died in hospital, and eight men were reported missing.

It is worthy of remark that the 1st, 2nd, and 3rd Battalions met in the streets of Ladysmith on 3rd of

* *Vide Official History of the South African War,* Vol. I, pp. 398-9.
† Now Brigadier-General and C.B.
‡ *Vide " Times" History of the South African War,* Vol. III, p. 324.
§ *Vide Official History of the South African War,* Vol. I, pp. 476-484.

March, 1900, when Sir Redvers Buller entered the town at the head of his army.

After the relief of Ladysmith, the 3rd Battalion with the Light Infantry Brigade of the 2nd Division took part in the advance through Northern Natal, in the passage of the Biggarsberg, and in the attacks on Botha Pass and Alleman's Nek, 8th–11th June. It entered Heidelberg at the end of June, 1900, and from that date until the end of October it was engaged in the neighbourhood of Standerton and Greylingstad protecting the railway. In November, 1900, Lieutenant-Colonel Bewicke-Copley was selected for command of a mobile column, which, till November the 19th, included his own 3rd Battalion. The Battalion subsequently occupied a line of blockhouses between Machadodorp and Dalmanutha, Eastern Transvaal, till the end of the war.

FOURTH BATTALION.

h BATTALION. The 4th Battalion was quartered at Cork during the earlier phases of the war, and was engaged in training and sending out reinforcements to a large extent of Mounted Infantry. It was not until December, 1901, that the Battalion, under the command of Lieutenant-Colonel E. W. Herbert,* sailed to Africa. Landing at Durban, it proceeded to Harrismith, O.R.C., where it constructed and occupied a line of blockhouses running west, and remained there until the conclusion of peace in June, 1902.

RIFLE RESERVE BATTALION.

IFLE RESERVE
ATTALION.
The Reserve Battalion, under the command of Major the Hon. E. J. Montagu-Stuart-Wortley, was organised at Pieter-Maritzberg, and composed of officers

---

* Now Colonel, C.B.

and reservists of The King's Royal Rifle Corps and of The Rifle Brigade, who were intended to re-inforce the battalions shut up in Ladysmith. It joined the 11th Brigade at Chieveley, Natal, in January, 1900, and took part in the operations of the 13th to the 27th of February, namely, Cingolo, Monte Christo, Hlangwane, Hart's Hill, and the final battle of Pieter's Hill. After the Relief of Ladysmith this improvised Battalion was broken up, and the officers and men of the Regiment were distributed between 1st and 2nd Battalions.

NINTH BATTALION.

This Militia Battalion of the Regiment, under the command of Lieutenant-Colonel William Cooke-Collis,* volunteered for active service, and, their services having been accepted, embarked for the seat of war in January, 1900. Landing at Cape Town on February 1st,† it proceeded at once to Naauwpoort, and took part in the operations round Colesburg. Leaving Naauwpoort in March, the Battalion was employed protecting the main line of communication and the reconstruction of the railway through the Free State in rear of *Lord Roberts'* army. It eventually took charge of the line between Vereeniging and Honing Spruit, where it remained for a year, during which its section of the line was never once cut by the enemy; this successful result was in a large measure due to the good work done by the company of Mounted Infantry raised from the Battalion.

9th BATTALI(
(NORTH COR)
MILITIA).

The Battalion returned home in August, 1901, and was disembodied.

---

* Now Colonel, C.M.G., and A.D.C. to the King.
† Two officers died on the voyage out.

THE MOUNTED INFANTRY OF THE KING'S ROYAL RIFLE CORPS.

Note.—The Mounted Infantry raised in the Regiment having played so distinguished a part in the campaign, it has been considered advisable for purposes of historical reference to record their services by battalions. The establishment of a Mounted Infantry Company was 5 officers and 142 other ranks, organized into four sections.

1st BATT. M.I.

A company was raised from the 1st Battalion in South Africa before the war ; it fought at Talana Hill (October the 20th, 1899), was in the DEFENCE OF LADYSMITH, and later with Buller's army until it arrived at Lydenburg in October, 1900. After this it was continually engaged in the Eastern Transvaal, until it joined the 25th Mounted Infantry in October, 1901 (*see below*). This Company lost twenty-five killed and thirty-three wounded during the war.

2nd BATT. M.I.

A Company was raised from the 2nd Battalion upon its arrival in Natal, which was left outside Ladysmith, and, joining Buller's army on the Tugela, took part in the campaign for the RELIEF OF LADYSMITH with *Dundonald's* Mounted Troops. After the relief this Company joined *Gough's* Mounted Infantry, and accompanied Buller's army up to Lydenburg, being subsequently engaged in the Eastern Transvaal, Zululand, and the Orange River Colony until the end of the war. The wastage in personnel was such that only two officers and twenty-nine others of the original company then remained, but the fact that twenty per cent. of the original horses, received in October, 1899, were still doing duty, constituted a notable record in horse management.

3rd BATT. M.I.

The 3rd Battalion contributed one section to " The Rifles' Company " of the 1st M.I. (*Vide 4th Battalion M.I.*).

A second section, formed in December, 1899, fought

with *Dundonald's* mounted troops in the RELIEF OF LADYSMITH, subsequently joining *Gough's* M.I. at Blood River Poort, where it was severely handled and its commander, Mildmay, was killed. This section, in October, 1901, was united with a third section raised in 1900, and joined the 25th M.I. in October, 1901 (*see below*), when the strength was raised to a full company.

The 4th Battalion contributed a section to " The Rifles' Company," under Captain Dewar, which, together with the section of the 3rd Battalion, and the two sections from the 3rd and 4th Battalions Rifle Brigade, formed one of the four companies composing the celebrated 1st M.I., organised and trained at Aldershot under *Lieutenant-Colonel E. A. H. Alderson* before the war. The " Rifles Company " was temporarily detached, and, landing at Port Elizabeth in November, 1899, joined the force under *Major-General Sir William Gatacre*, which was defeated at Stormberg on December the 12th, where it was mentioned for its gallant conduct in covering the retreat. The Company was then attached to *French's* Cavalry Division, and was at the battle of Paardeburg, where Captain Dewar was killed, and was also present at the surrender of Cronje on the 27th of February, Majuba Day. It then rejoined the 1st M.I.; and took part in the battles of Poplar Grove and Driefontein, and the entry into Bloemfontein (10th of March). It was at the surprise of Broadwood's Calvalry Brigade at Sannah's Post (31st of March), where it behaved with conspicuous gallantry, and it was at the relief of Wepener, and in the fighting near Thabanchu.

The 1st M.I. were then allotted to *Alderson's* Brigade with Hutton's* Mounted Troops, and took part in *Lord Roberts'* advance upon Pretoria on the 2nd May.

---

* *Vide* note p. 52.

The Company, therefore, was present in the actions of Brandfort, Vet River, Sand River, Kroonstadt, the Vaal River (27th of May), the battle of Doornkop, near Johannesburg (28th–29th of May), the actions at Kalkhoevel Defile, Six Mile Spruit (4th of June), and the entry into Pretoria (5th of June). It was similiarly engaged at the battle of Diamond Hill (11th of June); in the fighting south-east of Pretoria and at the action of Rietvlei (July the 16th); in the advance to and operations round Middelburg; in the battle of Belfast (24th of August, 1900); and in the march east from Dalmanutha, including the assault of the almost impregnable position of Kaapsche Hoop during the night of the 12th–13th of September.

From this time till the end of the war this Company was continually marching and fighting in the Orange River Colony and Cape Colony, pursuing De Wet, back again in the Transvaal, in countless forays and skirmishes, in the saddle night and day. When peace was declared it was at Vereeniging, whence it marched to Harrismith, and was absorbed into the Rifle Battalion of M.I. formed at that place.

The 4th Battalion also sent out two complete companies from Cork early in 1901, which were employed in the Transvaal, and subsequently joined the 25th M.I. in October of that year (*see below*).

25th (THE KING'S ROYAL RIFLE CORPS) MOUNTED INFANTRY BATTALION. On October the 18th, 1901, a complete Battalion of Mounted Infantry* was formed from the Regiment —an unique distinction—and consisted of:—

No. 1 Company 1st Battalion.
No. 2   ,,   4th Battalion.
No. 3   ,,   3rd Battalion.
No. 4   ,,   4th Battalion.

The Battalion was concentrated at Middelburg in the Transvaal, and was placed under the command

* For a more complete account, *vide Regimental Chronicle*, 1902, p. 94.

of Major C. L. E. Robertson-Eustace* until January, 1902, when he was succeeded by Major W. S. Kays.†

The Battalion thus organised was composed of officers and riflemen who had been in the field from the beginning of the war, and were therefore tried and experienced soldiers. It joined *Benson's*‡ column at Middelburg, a column of which it was said that no Dutchman dared sleep within thirty miles of its bivouac. The ceaseless activity and success of *Benson* eventually decided Louis Botha, the Boer Commander-in-Chief, to make a determined attempt to destroy his force. To achieve this purpose he collected nearly 2000 men, and by a skilful combination of his troops attacked the column while on the march near Bakenlaagte upon the 30th of October. By a rapid charge he overwhelmed the rear guard, captured two guns, killed *Benson*, and surrounded the column, but was eventually beaten off. The 25th M.I. fought with a stubborn courage, and by their sturdy gallantry kept the Boers at bay and gloriously upheld the traditions of the Regiment, losing in the action eleven men killed, five officers and forty-five men wounded.

Thus—stoutly fought out on both sides by mounted troops of this especial type—ended a fight which has been described as unique in the annals of war.§ The spirit of the Riflemen will best be understood from the lips of one of the wounded in this gallant fight, who remarked that " they were content if they had done their duty, and felt rewarded if their Regiment thought well of them."

The Mounted Infantry Battalion of the Regiment ended its short but brilliant career by taking part in

---

* Afterwards D.S.O. This promising officer died suddenly at Cairo, October 4th, 1908.
† Now Colonel.
‡ Colonel G. E. Benson, R.A., a leader of much distinction and initiative.
§ *Vide " Times" History of the War*, Vol. v.

all the great " drives " in the E. Transvaal and N.E. of the Orange Free State, and was finally at Greyling-stad when peace was declared on the 1st June, 1902.

RIFLE DEPOT.

RIFLE DEPOT. The Depot, under the command of Colonel Horatio Mends, was at Gosport throughout the war. A narrative of the work of the Regiment at this strenuous period would not be complete without grateful reference to the splendid service of administration, training, and equipment, so devotedly performed by the Colonel Commandant, his Staff, and the Company officers generally of the Rifle Depot.

The Adjutant was five times changed, but the Quarter - Master, Major Riley,* remained constant to his difficult duties throughout the whole of this trying ordeal.

It is stated that 4470 recruits joined the Depot, were trained, and passed to the various Battalions, while many thousands of Reservists were mobilized, equipped, clothed, and drafted for duty.

The work of discharge at the end of the war was not less severe, but there is no record of failure or of breakdown, and the success of the admirable system of administration was universally acknowledged.†

The Rifle Depot was moved back to Winchester on the 29th of March, 1903, after nine years of exile at Gosport caused by the re-building of the Barracks which had been destroyed by fire.

---

* Major T. M. Riley. Died 28th February, 1908. *Vide Regimental Chronicle,* 1907, p. 115.

† *Vide Regimental Chronicle,* 1903, pp. 202–207.

PART IV.

A RETROSPECT.

The preceding pages will have shown that the Regiment from its inception has possessed certain distinctive characteristics which are pre-eminently those required for making Light Infantry and Riflemen of the best type.

Raised in 1755, the Regiment, inspired by the genius of Henry Bouquet, early displayed that strong individuality, that self-reliant courage, and that ready initiative coupled with steady discipline, which won from the intrepid Wolfe himself the proud motto of *Celer et Audax.* ·In 1797, under the experienced command of Baron de Rottenburg, the famous 5th Battalion (Rifles) was raised as a special type of Light Troops. Thus the 5th Battalion of the Regiment, the first Rifle Corps of the British Army, revived those special qualities of the Royal Americans which had rendered the Regiment so renowned in its earlier years, and were destined to win imperishable fame throughout the Peninsular War.

After a long interval of peace the Regiment from 1836 to 1854 received a similar impetus at the hands of Molyneux and Dundas, and reaped a rich harvest of lasting honour and glory upon the Delhi Ridge by displaying the same supremely valuable characteristics which had distinguished it in America and in Spain. Again, from 1861–1873, under Hawley's commanding influence and inspiring skill, the Regiment, through the 4th Battalion, opened up a more rapid and elastic system of drill and tactics, a more intelligent treatment of the soldier, and the betterment of his life in barracks, of which the good effects are felt to-day not only in the Regiment but in the Army at large The qualities thus maintained for a century and a half, have borne in later years abundant fruit, of which the stubborn courage at the Ingogo fight, the calm discipline of the *Warren Hastings*, the eager valour of Talana Hill, and the impetuous assault up the slopes of the Twin Peaks are glorious examples.

To the same special qualities was due the inspiration which created the Mounted Infantry as a portion of the British Army, and it is to the officers and men of the 60th that the inception and success of that powerful arm is largely due.

Let the Riflemen of to-day, who read the deeds of their gallant comrades of the past, remember that if they are to maintain the traditions and increase still more the reputation of the famous Corps to which they belong, it can only be by cultivating the same spirit of ready self-sacrifice and unsparing devotion to duty, and by developing the same prompt initiative, steady discipline, and unflinching courage, which have ever been the secret of the Regiment's success.

Let each Rifleman also recollect that a distinguished Past is rather a reproach than a glory unless maintained by an equally distinguished Present, and developed, if possible, by an even more distinguished future.

MAP IV

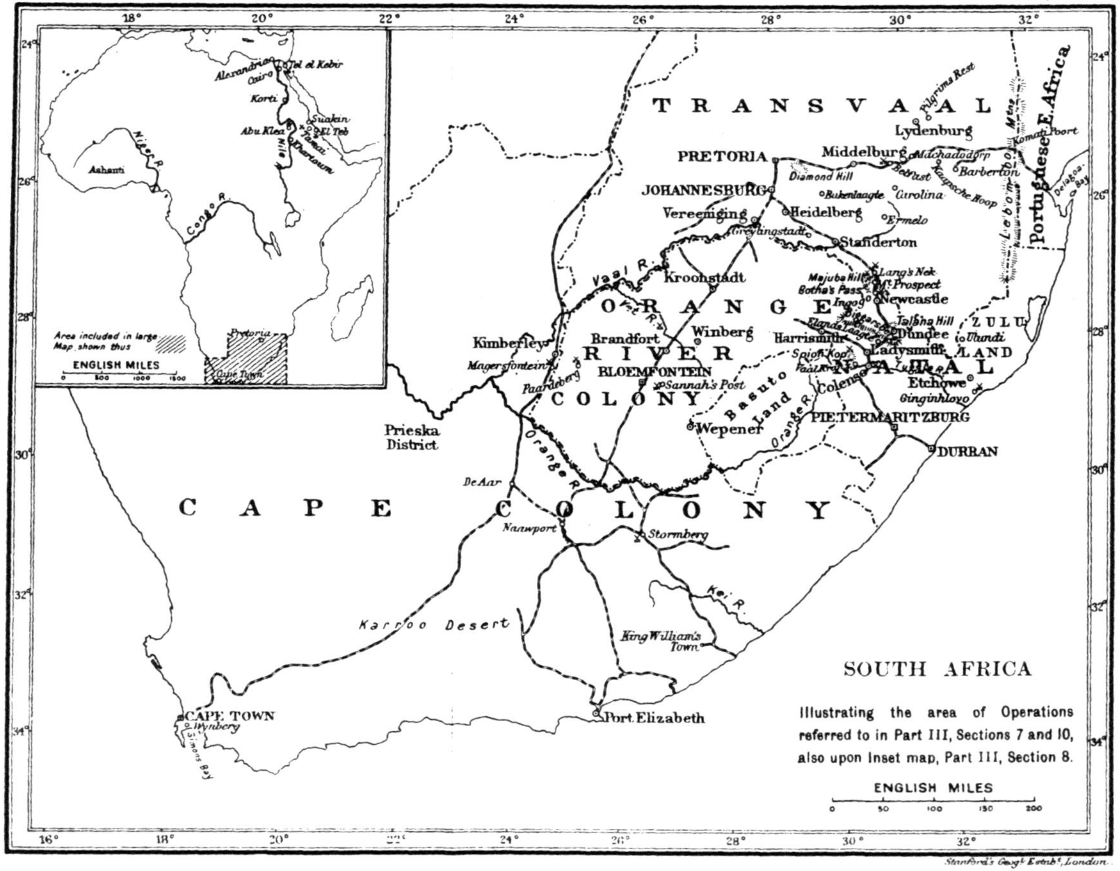
SOUTH AFRICA
Illustrating the area of Operations referred to in Part III, Sections 7 and 10, also upon Inset map, Part III, Section 8.
ENGLISH MILES
0 50 100 150 200
TRANSVAAL
ORANGE RIVER COLONY
CAPE COLONY
NATAL
ZULU LAND
Portuguese E. Africa
Basuto Land
PRETORIA
JOHANNESBURG
Vereeniging
Heidelberg
Standerton
Middelburg
Lydenburg
Pilgrims Rest
Machadodorp
Barberton
Belfast
Diamond Hill
Bukenlaagte
Carolina
Kaapsche Hoop
Ermelo
Komati Poort
Delagoa Bay
Lebombo
Greylingstadt
Kroonstadt
Vaal R.
Majuba Hill
Lang's Nek
Bothas Pass
Mt. Prospect
Ingogo
Newcastle
Talana Hill
Dundee
Ulundi
Harrismith
Ladysmith
Spion Kop
Colenso
Etchowe
Ginginhlovo
PIETERMARITZBURG
DURBAN
Winberg
Brandfort
BLOEMFONTEIN
Sannah's Post
Wepener
Kimberley
Magersfontein
Paardeberg
Prieska District
Orange R.
De Aar
Naauwport
Stormberg
Kei R.
King William's Town
Karroo Desert
Port Elizabeth
CAPE TOWN
Wynberg
Simons Bay
Alexandria
Cairo
Tel el Kebir
Korti
Suakin
El Teb
Abu Klea
Tamai
Khartoum
Nile
Niger R.
Ashanti
Congo R.
Pretoria
Cape Town
Area included in large Map shown thus
ENGLISH MILES
0 500 1000 1500
Stanford's Geog! Estab!, London.

Lightning Source UK Ltd.
Milton Keynes UK
07 June 2010

155265UK00001B/128/A